Make Love to Her Soul, Not Her Flesh

Make Love to Her Soul,
Not Her Flesh

Minister Stephen L. Green

Contents

Preface — xi

1. Security — 1
2. Adoration — 7
3. The Indirect Motive — 13
4. Love — 19
5. She Is Your You — 27
6. Diffuse the Situation — 33
7. Truth — 39
8. Why the soul? — 45
9. You Have To Know God — 49
10. Now is time — 55

Shirley Mae Berry

April 22, 1945 – February 15, 2020

My mother, Shirley Mae Berry, was a beautiful person, inside and out. She was a hardworking, single mother of five children. Three beautiful daughters and two handsome sons. She was also a professional seamstress, and a caring person. This particular dedication is a bit personal. Not personal because I am dedicating this book, my first, to my mother, but personal because of one of the reasons I believe I decided to write this book. My entire bloodline on my mother's side of the family was filled with gifts and talents that were never used. Anointings and blessings that were never tapped into. With me writing this book, I am the first to step out in faith, using the gift that God has given me. And for me, this is an eternally big step. One that I am proud to take. My mom had a desire to own her own business. A few years before she passed away, I had the honor of hosting a business expo that allowed her to get her very first experience of business exposure. Now that she's gone, I know that she's smiling down on us, and I personally aim to see her smile. Without my mother, I wouldn't be here.

So, to my mother, Shirley Mae Berry, this book is dedicated to you, with love. I will always love you and I will see you again!

Special dedication

Before I begin, let me just say, because I used the word "special", I'm not taking away from the other dedications. My mom and dad were very special to me, and always will be. The other person in this dedication is still very much alive. This dedication is to my firstborn, my daughter, Dija. My daughter and I were robbed of a bonding relationship together. I won't go into details, but I missed your first steps, prom, and graduation. There are so many things I've missed in your life. If I could go back and change things, I would. I want you to know that although I wasn't physically there, there was not a day that went by that I didn't think about you. I have always loved you, and this special dedication is to you, baby girl. I also want you to know that Daddy loves you now and always will. I truly hope that this book touches you emotionally and shows you who you really are. Tell my grandbaby I love her!

Preface

Why Make Love To Her Soul, Not Her Body? Honestly, I don't even know. One day, the Holy Spirit began to minister to me about eternal things pertaining to a woman. I found the information both interesting and intriguing. Interesting because our whole lives, we think we have an understanding about something, but Isaiah 55:8 says God's thoughts are totally different. The complete opposite, if you ask me. As I began to meditate on the revelation that God was giving me, some points stood out louder than others.

The first point being are there men out there who really don't know how to make love to a woman the way God intended. If God's ways are truly different, and I can personally attest to the truth that they are, then that is an area that we have not been operating in the way God intended. Another point that I found very interesting is that there are women who wonder, or have an eternal desire to know what it feels like to be made love to physically, spiritually, emotionally, and mentally.

Do they wonder if there is something else other than what they have already experienced? Although other questions arose, these two stood out the most to me. They stood out the most because they showed me from God's point of view, that there is a lack of knowledge on both the male and the female side of God's original plans for mankind. The very thing that people perish for. The lack of knowledge. These revelatory encounters happened for a couple of days. Now, God tells us in his word that everything he does is for a purpose and a reason, so I inquired about the purpose and the reason.

I'll never be a woman, so this would only be knowledge for me. Thus comes *Make Love To Her Soul, Not Her Flesh*. He showed me an avenue to get this knowledge to those who need it. To be perfectly honest, I've never made love to a woman's soul. But for me, after receiving God's revelation, I've learned that there are levels to a woman that even a husband will never know if he does not know how to love a woman right. Prayerfully, the revelation that God has revealed will equip his people to step up to the plate.

For the man, to learn and understand how to truly make love to a woman the way God intended. For the woman, to learn her eternal value, and to present to her a measuring stick, so she will always know if she is being loved the way God intended. Now let's learn how to make love to her soul!

Chapter 1

Security

When She Is Secure In Her Heart, Mind, and Spirit, The Body Is The Reward!

I must be honest with you. To me, this seems to be one of the most important chapters in this book. As a former United States Marine (USMC), I've seen many parts of the world. As a steward of three children, I must say, that I've seen a relationship or two. But I can honestly say, if I would have known the information in this book, I don't think there would be a path of broken relationships in my life. This one chapter has opened my closed eyes.

When God began to minister to me about this particular subject, I really began to see that a woman has a quality from God, that is there, and it operates beyond her abilities and her control. I don't think the average woman knows that this particular quality is at work in her being. Now when one thinks about the word security, the word that comes to my mind, for some strange reason is vault. I mean, how hard is it to include in one's sentence or vocabulary, the words security and vault. The interesting thing is how God connected the words security and vault in relation to the woman.

Let's take a good look. We now know and fully understand that the word of God teaches us that the divine trinity consists of three beings, the Father, the Son, and the Holy Spirit. I have come to the full understanding that when it comes to a woman feeling any type of security in any type of relationship, there's only one way and one way only that it's going to happen. Before a man can make a woman feel fully secure, he must first know how. Now let's see why I mentioned the trinity. Before a woman can begin to feel secure in any relationship, she must have three pieces of her inner self completely put together.

Not only do they need to be completely put together, but they must also be in complete sync. Because of the nature of the woman, this three-piece puzzle must never be broken. If you have any knowledge or experience putting puzzles together, you know that each piece has its own place. The one unique thing about a puzzle is the pieces either fit or they don't. There is no in between. Now let's understand and discover the mystery behind the puzzle in a woman. We already know that a woman is an emotional creature by nature.

Although they are created with many emotions, there are three areas in a woman's being, where her emotions will always be at their peak. The thing about a woman's emotions is they hold certain keys to different levels of their lives. But, for right now, let's look at everything that deals with the security of a woman.

When a woman doesn't feel secure, the thing that she feels is cautiousness. Because a woman is an emotional creature, we understand that to a woman, caution is an emotion. Yes, caution is a real-life emotion. Just as she does to every other emotion, a woman will also respond to caution. When a woman feels cautious in any way, her dominant nature kicks in immediately. Her dominant nature is protection. She feels that she must now protect her every possession. She now lives in an unseen world of defense. Every barrier is up because she feels she now must protect everything that is dear to her. She doesn't see the need to let her guard down because at this point, the only person she trusts is herself. She will go through her everyday life knowing her security is in her own ability, however weak or strong, to protect herself and her possessions. She has the mindset what does she need a man for?

Now let's look back at that puzzle. In order for a woman to feel the security that she needs to feel, there are three different areas that she needs heavily guarded. The first area that the woman needs to feel secure in is her mind. In any given situation, a woman must have the mental peace that whatever the subject matter is, it will not affect her mentally.

A woman must have a full understanding of what's being discussed, what is going on, and what direction to move in. Any questions that she has must be answered with answers that bring peace and enforces security. She can't have any intellectual apprehensions, or she won't have a peace of mind about what is being asked of her. No peace of mind for her means there's no mental security, so she will not budge. When a woman doesn't have mental security, she can't produce. The second area where a woman needs to be secure in is her heart. Now this is a much bigger issue than the mind because the heart is the computer, (CPU), central processing unit, of all the emotions she has and processes.

Her heart is the ground that harvests every emotional seed. When it comes to the security of her heart, if she feels the slightest alert, her heart will automatically shut down. The scary thing is the shut down can happen without her knowing. No matter how hard one tries, they will not be able to get around her shut down heart. In order for her heart to feel secure, the man must understand that every emotion, question, concern, if, what if, and how about, has to be completely settled. She must have a complete peace in her heart from every concern. Now as much as this sounds like the security of the mind, there's a big difference. The big difference is the shut down in her heart is automatic. In most cases, she can pretty much regulate her mind, but she has no control over the way her heart shuts down. There can be no waves in the ocean of her heart. Smooth sailing means a secure heart. The last area that a woman needs to feel secure in is her spirit.

Now, this last area is by far, the most important area. Some call this an element of a woman's intuition. A woman, as well as a man, has a certain piece of God that is always in full operation.

There are times where we can know every natural detail about a situation, but be completely blind or ignorant about that exact same situation in the spirit. We can know something is wrong, but just can't see it. Have you ever heard anyone say, I don't know what it is, but I can feel something is wrong. The knowing is not in the mind or the heart, but in the spirit. The woman has to know and have a peace in her spirit that whatever is being asked of her is also pleasing to God. If a red flag goes off in her spirit, to her that's an unction from God himself, alerting her that there's something wrong that she can't see with her natural eyes.

Even if she doesn't know what is wrong, when a woman doesn't feel secure in her spirit, it will take God, and God alone, to assure her because now her spirit is troubled. Man can offer his words of encouragement and lend a listening ear for comfort, but it will take God to reach her spiritually. Once the heart, mind, and spirit of the woman are in complete alignment, the security of her vault is completed. She now has the security that she needs to feel completely safe!

Chapter 2

Adoration

The Eyes Of Adoration

Talk about interesting. This is one of those chapters where the average woman will say how does he know so much about being a woman. To answer that question, I would have to say that the Holy Spirit is an excellent teacher. He definitely knows the nature of the woman. We must first understand some things. I've already stated a woman is an emotional creature by nature. The one thing that I didn't mention was her emotions come with what I would call sensors. Although men and women both have emotions, when it comes to the woman, these emotions feed into every area of her life. Unlike us men, it's pretty much impossible for a woman not to see things through the eyes of her emotions. Now let's see how the word adoration ties into emotions. Let's look at a typical situation. A husband and wife are doing some remodeling. One day they go to a Home Depot to purchase some supplies. The one thing that will always happen is the man will see the whole picture, know what is needed and proceeds from there. Whether that particular store has all that is needed, or he makes the required number of stops to acquire the necessary supplies.

The woman on the other hand, has not only started a completely different process, but has also seen the project through a completely different set of eyes. I call them the eyes of adoration. A woman has what I would say, some sort of gift. They have the ability where they can look through their eyes of adoration and see the complete value of a thing. While I'm not saying that a man has no vision, I'm simply saying the woman has this special ability. In this home remodeling project, we see what's needed and what the finished product will be. She sees, not only the finished product, but something else that she only sees and can explain.

At this point, I'm sure you're wondering, what does this ability have anything to do with adoration. I am so glad you asked that question. I've come to learn and understand that a woman loves to spend quality time alone by herself. Now when I was much younger than I am now, I used to think that such a request was rather rude. A subtle way to escape and cheat. Boy was I wrong! Since a woman is emotional by nature, they need alone time to be emotional. Now I know that sounds crazy, but they do. This time is extremely important to them because this is their time to be one thing and one thing only, a woman.

Not a mom, not a wife, not a friend, simply a woman. She needs to breathe as a woman, woosa as a woman, and meditate as a woman. Before she became a mom, wife, or any other title, she was a woman.

A place of freedom in her mind that means the world to her. Now although several things happen when she is in this place, the thing that stands out to me is the very thing that I am writing about. During this time alone, she spends a great deal of that time adoring herself. Now this is not pride and this is not lust. This is her time to visually see the value in herself, so she adores herself. She spends a lot of time adoring her body. A woman literally knows every curve on her body. She knows every spot, wrinkle, and blemish. She knows the direction the hair on her legs lay down. Through her eyes of adoration, she is able to see the true value of herself. The thing as men, we need to understand that it's during this time there is nothing negative in her eyes. Even if she has a scar or bruise, that scar or bruise has value to her. It's a part of her body, so it too, has value. It deserves respect, simply because of the price she paid to get that scar or bruise. Adoration!

Another thing, we as men need to understand is, if adoration is a part of the woman's supernatural DNA, then we must make it a part of our everyday thinking process. That's if we truly want to make love to her soul. This alone time is also a learning time. It's during this time where she learns to love herself, inwardly and outwardly. Now here's the female perspective. When a man adores a woman, he notices everything about her. Another perspective of the woman is this is also a learning time for him. A time to prove if she is really on his mind. She needs her emotional ears soothed with those things he has learned about her on his own. She wants to know was he really adoring her or lusting after his own physical desires. She already knows that once that physical desire is met, those lustful thoughts will fade away.

She is more interested in the adoration because of the volume it speaks to her. During any learning process, the thing that happens is one lets down their intellectual walls so that they can properly receive and understand what is being learned. When we truly adore a woman, we are telling that woman that we are willing to let down our intellectual walls and trust what we are learning on our own about her. She loves the fact that the man is willingly putting in the time to get to physically know her without one, her opening her mouth, and two, he has learned things about her without having touched her. To the woman, that is called intimate love. A love that carries a lot more weight than that of physical attraction. This is telling the woman that you are interested in her and not what you want from her.

The dangerous thing about adoration is it puts at a limit on things by always demanding the truth about her. We can't get a tip about her from someone else, and then try to pass if off as something we learned while adoring her. She wants you to notice that little bump behind her ear that she has not been too successful at hiding. Not stalking or crossing any type of psychological lines, but humbly noticing an imperfection that still makes her beautiful. She wants him to know that she struggles with her weight, but still acts as if nothing is wrong. Where is the value in telling her how fine she is? Where is the value in telling her how pretty she is? Now, please don't in any way misunderstand what I am saying. These things are exceptionally important for a woman to hear, but they are also the most common things that she hears. To the woman, if you are truly adoring her, you will notice things that will make her say to herself, he really is paying attention to me. Another perspective of the woman is it's during this time of adoration when the man whose eye she has caught, can show her his difference between adoration and lust. Now the funny thing is we will never have to tell her which one is which because she will know. She has learned her value so she will automatically know if she is being lusted after or if she is being truly adored. Adoration or lust.

Chapter 3

The Indirect Motive
The Shift Of Purpose

I think I'll start this chapter with "wow"! Not taking anything away from the other chapters, but this particular chapter, I found extremely interesting because of the title. God had given me the name of each chapter, but this one had me eager to write. As I wrote down the word motive, I couldn't understand why God would use such a word to describe a woman. Once he began to minister to me, it all began to make sense. I can honestly and truthfully say that when it comes to true love, a woman will always have a motive, and now that I know her true motive, I am perfectly fine with it. Let's start right here. As we already know, everything that God does is for a purpose and a reason. The word tells us that everything that God created was good, then he rested. His word also says that when a man finds a wife, he finds a good thing.

So, here's the thing, everything that he created was already declared good. So why go a step further and call the wife a good thing? Was he referring to something specific? Good question. Remember, purpose and reason. Now here's where it gets interesting. God took a rib from Adam. Why the rib? Every rib in the human body serves a purpose. I'm not speaking of the overall rib cage itself, but each individual rib has a purpose. Each rib was created with a purpose. Now, let's look at the shift of purpose. When God took the rib from Adam, he never took away the purpose of the rib. So even out of Adam's body, Adam's rib still had a purpose. So, if we really catch the shift, we should see what really happened. The rib never lost its purpose, so when God created the woman, she was automatically created with purpose.

The woman was created with what I would call an eternal switch. Purpose! The woman didn't create herself, so she has absolutely nothing to do with how she was created or what was placed down on the inside of her. Purpose! Now what does purpose have to do with motive? I'm glad you proposed such an interesting question. I think I just might have the answer. To understand such a question, we must first look at the purpose. As we learned earlier, her purpose is like a switch that she can't control. We also need to understand that unless God turns that switch off, which I seriously doubt he will, she will always have that switch on. Basically, the woman is being driven by something she can not control. The reason she can not do anything about it is because it's eternal.

She would probably choose to operate a different way, but as we discussed earlier, she didn't create herself. Because we now understand that the woman is driven by what we know now as purpose, we understand that the woman in a sense, really does have a motive. But we can not charge her for her motive because we now know and understand that her motive comes with an eternal switch that she can not turn off.

She's operating on an eternal circuit that forever runs. Purpose! Now let's evaluate purpose and motive a little bit more. In order to do that, we need to understand the nature, or design of the purpose that has been placed down in her. Her nature is who she really is. If I had to use one word to describe the true nature of a woman, it would definitely be incubator. If I had to place a label that suited the eternal purpose, the label would again say incubator. A woman has the same operation going on in her being that an incubator has when it's in operation. The reason I compare the nature of the woman to an incubator is because of the common denominator known as life. A perfectly functioning incubator has the distinct ability to contribute to what we know as human life.

A woman has the exact same element. She is the carrier of life. A more detailed word that further describes her is nurturer. Her true nature is all about producing and nurturing life. Not only producing life, but contributing to the continuation of life. This is who she is, and this is what she does. Driven by eternal purpose, a woman is basically a giver by nature. This is her true motive or her unseen motive. Now let's see what the woman's motive has to do with a man. When a woman is in a relationship with a man, her true nature becomes a part of that relationship. The incubator in her is always in operation. Even though an operating incubator contributes to life, it cannot produce anything unless something is first placed in it. The incubator is automatically programmed to produce whatever it is programmed to produce.

The nature of the woman is the exact same way. She is automatically programmed to produce. The beautiful thing about this is the incubator doesn't know its purpose, but a woman does. She may not want to be who she is, but she can not stop the operation that goes on in her. She knows she has the inner ability to produce life. When she is in a relationship, she will always have an indirect motive because it comes with the nature of who she is.

Secret is, she knows. Now because she knows her value, and knows that she is a giver of life, in her heart, she wants to use her incubator to bring life to her relationship. She wants to be used in the capacity that she was created in. If you really pay attention to a woman who has truly fallen in love, she wants to hear all about the current and future plans of the person she has fallen in love with.

Now that she has fallen in love, she wants to be involved in literally everything he has going on in his life. She has an indirect motive. The incubator in her is crying out for something to be placed in it. The difference here is the incubator doesn't have any emotions, but the woman does. The eternal incubator is doing what is designed to do. Because the woman carries an indirect motive, she craves to give life to everything that person has going on. Her motive is to see life be pumped into everything that needs life.

She nourishes every idea he has and tries with everything in her physical power to bring those ideas into manifestation. She sees the value in his dreams, and she has the heart to put in the physical labor just to sec his dreams come true. Her eternal incubator is in full throttle. Now we know in a normal situation involving a person with a motive. We also know and understand the meaning of the word motive. So, ninety nine percent of the time a person with a motive has some type of hidden agenda. In any conversation, or in any of her actions, the woman is not trying to hide her agenda. Her motive is very clear, and she makes it perfectly known. To be the woman who I am, and to do what God needs me to do. That's her real motive!

Chapter 4

Love

Moved To A City Called Love

One of the most commonly used words that tends to have so many different meanings to so many different people. Because I now realize that a woman is an emotional creature by creation, I fully understand that love is also an emotion. For a woman, love works a bit different than it does for a man. For years, in my life, I noticed a pattern that under any circumstances did not change. I've seen it in real life. I've seen it on television, and still, it plays out the exact same way every time. When a woman is truly honest with herself and realizes that she has fallen in love, her whole world as far as security changes.

The thing that I've noticed every time is when a woman first falls in love, she feels the need to have a detailed conversation about the truth of her falling in love. I used to wonder why there had to be a conversation, or why we had to sit down and hold a conversation about her falling in love. I love you too, but we don't need to sit down and talk about it. "BOY, WAS I WRONG". But think about it. If a woman makes up her mind that there is something she needs to talk about, you can rest assured, it's extremely important to her.

But let's be realistic for a minute, how much can one talk about falling in love. For a woman, falling in love is a major milestone in her journey called life. It doesn't matter how many times she has been in love, it's the falling that concerns her. When a woman falls in love, she doesn't just fall in love. A woman knows how to evaluate every necessary precaution before falling in love. For a woman, in her emotional stance, falling in love is quite similar to, if we can be visual for a second, a woman standing on the edge of a tall building, pondering on getting ready to jump. While she's standing on the edge, a million thoughts and emotions are racing through her mind.

I've come to the understanding that this is quite the experience for a woman. When a woman falls in love, the first thing she wants to do is talk to the person who she has fallen in love with. The reason she wants to talk is because the person whom she has fallen in love with needs to be made aware of what has changed in her life.

The thing I literally love about this concept is the woman's perception in the element of having fallen.

Not to be graphic in a negative way, but when one jumps from a certain place, no matter how high, the only thing that this person knows and feels is the wind itself. God revealed the exact same concept happens when a woman truly falls in love. We're already aware of the fact that many say they've fallen in love, but have no idea of what real love is. But when a woman truly falls in love, she has done just that. She has willingly chosen to allow herself to jump off that emotional cliff called love.

She has questioned and answered every emotion she has in detail. She has evaluated every possible positive and negative scenario, and provided the best possible solutions. She has looked at everyone else's feelings, position, and input. She has talked to her parents, best friend, and anyone else who she values and has taken their advice to heart. Once she searches deep, deep within and truthfully finds no more no's, she sees no reason not to fall, so she jumps. Now here is where it gets interesting for the vessel whom she has fallen in love with.

Everyone knows that love is important and an important subject matter. For a woman, the word important is really an understatement. Remember we discussed when a woman truly falls in love, one of the first things she does is have a sit down conversation? When anyone summons someone else to have a sit-down conversation, it's more than important. It's serious. True love to a woman is very serious and important. Now, lets go a little further. There's a reason why the woman zeros in on the very person she fell in love with. She could have chosen someone like a best friend, co-worker, relative, or anyone else to talk to.

But now her choice is made and she's in love. The reason she chooses the person she has fallen in love with is because the person she has fallen in love with has now suddenly become that wind. At this point, she is literally off the cliff. Just as the wind would be the connection in a real fall, she now sees the person that she has fallen in love with as her immediate connection. All she sees is him. The only voice she really wants to hear, other than the voice of God, is his.

The only thing that now catches her eyes is his presence. Her heart has now become consumed with wanting to spend her every moment in his presence. She now spends a great deal of intellectual time coming up with ways to please him. He has become her wind and now she has a goal. She now has something that is very valuable to her. Love! He has become the sparkle in her eyes. There's an old saying that clearly stands out in this particular chapter. He has become the wind beneath her wings.

This is a feeling she has never experienced before, so her focus of attention from this point on, is to navigate through the wind. She's going to do whatever she needs to do to protect her newfound wind. Some women describe this new feeling as a drug, and some women have expressed to some men being their drug. She's in love. Now, let's look at this sit down conversation. What is the real nature of the conversation, and why is it so serious? Now that she has fallen in love, she has become secure in his love. This new love is now a part of her security.

She has given up every precaution, so she now needs him to fully understand her new position. She needs him to know that outside of God, she has given him everything. She has found him worthy of the space in her mind, the place in her heart, and the key to her soul. She needs to talk to him because he needs to fully understand what's at stake for her. She is now full of all types of butterflies, emotions, questions, and physical cravings. Her body is now doing things it wasn't doing before. She's on a new high that only he can fulfill. Now, this may not seem like something serious enough to have a conversation about, but for her, it is. It is for one main reason, and that reason is fear. In this new place in her life, there's no one there but them. Although she still has those normal people around her physically, the only person that literally exists in her world of new found love is him.

She must fulfill the need within herself to let him know that this new place is scary for her, and she needs to be reassured that there is no need to fear. Now that's easier said than done for the man, but for her, it's a milestone. She needs him to understand that she has detached herself from everything emotionally, and now all the emotions she has are now all directed at him. The biggest emotion, which to her is trump, that is running rampant right now is trust. She needs him to understand what it is like for her. For her, its like she has emotionally moved to another city or country, and the only person she knows is him.

Anyone that picks up and moves to a completely new city, state, or country, completely alone, knows how scary such a move can be. Well, she packed up and moved to love. Such a move automatically brings a serious battle with fear. Because one understands this, one would really have to understand that the woman is currently experiencing the same type of fear. True love is now her new city, state, and country. The word of God tells us in detail what love is and what love is not.

If you really pay attention to a woman who has fallen in love, you will see literally everything God decrees. I love how true genuine love brings out the best in a woman. A woman, to me, who has really fallen in love, gives off the sweetest odor of humility. When a woman realizes that she has truly fallen in love, her vision of value immediately changes. Now don't get me wrong, the woman never sees herself of no value. But when a woman falls in love, she now sees the value that she brings to the table.

Her love is valuable and her love is genuine. Her love comes with no attachments and no hidden agendas. In its truest form, God created the genuine love of a woman to nurture the relationship that she is in!

Chapter 5

She Is Your You

Equally Yoked

The title of this particular chapter is rather strange. But it will definitely make sense as your understanding is enlightened. Let's take a trip to the book of Genesis. The very beginning. The word of God tells us that God formed man from the dust of the earth. The formation of man was basically a shell until God blew breath into him. It was then man became a living soul. Now at this point, Adam is an exact replica of God. Basically, as the word declares it, Adam was a little god. He was only placed in an Earth suit so that he could identify and co-exist in the natural world. He was given dominion and authority to rule over the earth. Now let's go a little deeper. After God finished his other work, he created the woman.

We can safely look at the word woman to mean in a sense, man with a womb, or if you prefer a spiritual meaning, a carrier of life. Keep the understanding, or revelation carrier of life in the front of your mind. Now, as I look at the process of creation, and as I think back to the book of Ecclesiastes, something clearly stands out to me that arouses an eternal question. A question that can only be answered by God. In the book of Ecclesiastes, God tells us that he does everything for a purpose and a reason. In looking at the woman's creation process, I wondered why was the creation process different. What was the eternal reason for creating the man differently from the woman?

Because I understand that there is a purpose for every-thing that God does, I understand that even though Adam and Eve were together, they were each created for a specific reason or purpose. Why did God take a natural piece of Adam to create Eve? Why didn't he create Eve with the same breath of life? Why not use an Earthen shell? At that time Adam hadn't fallen yet, so he was still all spirit. I truly believe God could have performed the same creation process, but he didn't. Why? By taking a natural piece of Adam to create Eve, I believe that somehow Adam's specific purpose would be the giver of life. That was his purpose. Considering he named all the animals, I'd say it's safe to call him the giver of life. So, if the man is the giver of life, I believe it's safe to say that the woman is the carrier of life.

Although Eve was created more on the natural side, she was still created before Adam fell. So technically, she was all spirit as well. She possessed a certain ability to produce life that God knew Adam needed both naturally and spiritually. Thus, being called Adam's help meet. Even before Adam fell, and after, God never put Eve in a position of complete rule and authority. Her very first position in the kingdom of God was to be a help meet to Adam.

Now most look at this term as meaning a little helper, but in this case, once we understand the position of helper, we'll soon understand that there's nothing small about it.

Even though Adam was all spirit before he fell, he was placed in a natural Earth suit, so he, being all spirit, had natural responsibilities that had to be naturally done. Eve, who was also spirit, was responsible for helping Adam carry out the natural element of God's spiritual vision. Although in an Earth suit, Adam's vision was still spiritual. Adam's mind was literally all spirit, so he needed the natural side of Eve for help. It was apparent or obvious to Adam that he knew God's vision, and Eve helped him carry out the natural side. Now let's go a little deeper. Because Eve came specifically from Adam, she was a part of him. Eve came directly from the inside of Adam, so whether Adam wanted her to or not, she knew him, and she knew how he thought.

She knew his heart, his emotions, and how he operated on a daily basis. Eve was basically a replica of Adam. A natural replica of a spiritual being. She was successful at helping Adam run the kingdom because she was him in a sense. She knew God's vision and was created to help Adam carry it out. As I began to understand more and more, I realized that as a man created by God, there has to be an Eve that fits the rib that belongs to me. Now I know many use this statement lightly, but its supernatural genetics. The interesting thing about a woman in general is she wants to help. She's created to help. When a woman is truly found by her Adam, there is an undeniable connection between the two that can not be explained or resisted by either.

A true Eve understands the man better than he understands himself. She wants and needs him to understand that she knows her roll and is dedicated to seeing the vision that God has given her Adam come to past. She will think like her Adam would, and make decisions in the same manner that he would. She needs to see the vision manifest, because although she is committed to her roll as a helper, she still needs to see God pleased. When we fully understand God's plan, we begin to understand that in a nutshell, Eve was Adam's Adam. Women today want and need to know that their meaning is greater than the bedroom.

Their meaning is greater than getting a job and helping pay the bills. Although many won't admit it, and even more don't understand that there is something down on the inside of every woman to want to be a part of God's vision. It only takes the right Adam to come along and present it to her. Every woman wants to be pleasing to God. When you allow a woman to truly be herself in God, you give her the opportunity to please God, carry the vision, and to ultimately in a sense, be you. She is your you!

Chapter 6

Diffuse the Situation

The True Art Of Communication

Diffuse the situation was kind of tricky to write. The reason I say tricky is because the average woman might not want this particular part of their nature revealed. I actually hesitated on writing this chapter until God instructed me otherwise. He said the wrong woman would not want this information revealed because of cruel intentions and hidden motives. He said the right woman wants this information revealed because her intentions are purely to be loved the right way. Thus, giving me the green light to write. Now, let's go further. The reason I was hesitant to write this chapter is because of the specific illustration in content.

If I had to put into words how I want to illustrate the woman in this particular chapter, it would be simply a bag. In a sense, in plain sight, the creation of the woman can be looked at as a bag of emotions. Everything about the natural creation and make up of the woman is tied to some type of emotion. When it comes to us men, some words to us are just words. Words with impactful meanings, but just words. To a woman, those exact words are tied to an emotion. Rather directly or indirectly, a woman is flesh, so she can teach and train herself to display a hard exterior in difficult situations and full of emotions on the inside. Displaying a hard exterior is only a way of hiding her true emotions and avoiding the truth.

Sometimes women are emotional within themselves, and have no idea or clue as to why they are so emotional at that specific moment. Men don't dwell in the emotional department and are not created that way. Men touch base with the reality of their emotions based on what is going on and move accordingly. Because women are emotional creatures by nature, it is hard for them to easily put their emotions to rest. Although every woman is different, a woman knows how to process each in its own lane and perspective. Once men become fully knowledgeable of exactly how emotional a woman can be, they will then learn the true art of communication between a man and a woman.

Now, let's take a deeper look at that emotional bag. Or do we say a bag of emotions? The one thing about a bag is its contents can be surprising sometimes. Let's say one went shopping for a variety of apples and one comes home with a full bag of apples. The bag is full of different colored apples. Now at this point, even if I don't immediately know the color, the one thing I do know for sure is when I reach into that bag, an apple is coming out. Now let's say that person lets some time go by and some of the apples go bad.

Regardless of how much time has passed, and what condition some of the apples are in, there is one thing that has not changed and will not change. Every time the hand goes into that bag, an apple is coming out. Hopefully by now you've gotten the revelation concerning the bag. Now let's tie those apples to those emotions. Good and bad, a woman is filled with emotions. The key to the art of communication is knowing how to successfully navigate through the bag and pull out the right apple. Now don't get me wrong, no one is perfect, so this type of navigation won't be easy considering the fact that men are not emotional creatures.

This particular type of navigation is always a challenge because you never know what emotion or apple is going to get picked. Basically, this is a learning process that does not happen overnight. Here is where I must be blunt to the male reader. If you're in a relationship with a woman, that woman is your bag of apples. Now when I make that statement, I'm not speaking from a perspective of any type of ownership, but merely your responsibility to work with the apples that come in the bag. Now, let's get a little bit more realistic with those apples and tie them to those emotions. First, understand that most men don't like to waste money.

There will be times when he reaches into that bag and pulls out an apple that has perfect appearance on the outside, but issues on the inside. There will be also times when the apple has some issues on the outside surface, but still perfectly fine on the inside.

There will be times when there is absolutely nothing wrong with the apple at all. Let's call those apples good days. Now let's go back to the other two scenarios. Those two scenarios produce two things automatically. Those two things are worth and work. One who does not like to waste money looks at the imperfect apples with value. And instead of discarding the apples, one would simply remove the outer issues and enjoy the inside, or one would discard the middle and enjoy the apple as a whole. Either way, it's a little work for the one who sees the worth in the remaining parts of the apple. Now let's take it a step further.

There will be emotions in the woman from both previously discussed scenarios. Those emotions from the perspective of the woman, automatically produces those same two words, work and worth. Now if you noticed, I used the same two words, but used them in a different order. I stated those two words in the exact manner of how the woman looks at the situation. She knows that she is not perfect, and she knows she has her outer or inner bruisings. Some women have both in the woman's eyes. She wants to know if she is worth the work. She knows that if he still wants to enjoy that specific apple, he'll have to take the time to cut away the bad parts.

Now in her case she knows the man won't actually be doing any cutting, but allowing God to do the cutting while he patiently waits. Now let's diffuse the situation. Let's take a look at those bad spots and bruisings. These spots and bruisings are more than likely tied to some type of negative emotion. An area in her life that does not produce positive results. When you get to one of these emotions, or bad spots present the positive for the nega-tive. If she is crying, make her laugh. If she is down, pick her up. If she is afraid, make her feel safe. If she is worried, be her peace. Diffuse the situation! By diffusing the situation, you are taking away the power of the nega-tive impact from the bad spots or bruises on the apple. No Power. No confusion!

Chapter 7

Truth

Big Difference Between The Truth And
A Fact

How do I begin this chapter? With such a powerful topic, where would one begin to speak? In all the years I have been ministering, the one thing that I constantly saw as a pattern was a struggle with two things. One, people really don't want to hear the truth, and two, people don't want to have to deal with it once it's put out there. The word of God tells us that the truth shall make you free. Question number one, make is a forcible word, so why does freedom have to be forced? Question number two, why didn't God say the fact shall make you free? Could there be a difference between the truth and a fact? Jesus said *"I am the way, the truth and the life."* He also said that he would send back the spirit of truth. One must completely understand that there is a big difference between a fact and the truth. One might still disagree, so let's look at a story in the word of God. We all know the story of the three Hebrew boys who were thrown into the fire because they refused to bow down and worship one of the world's kings.

Now let's look at the facts first. They were bound by their hands so they couldn't free themselves. The fire was fueled so it was meant to burn for a long time. There were thousands of witnesses that witnessed three men be bound up and set on fire. The king stood there with armed guards to ensure that the men burned alive. Now if all of the men had actually burned in the fire, then everything I mentioned would be the truth instead of facts. Now let's look at truth regarding the same story. The first truth is there were four men in the fire instead of three. There was another fire burning inside of the already burning fire. The truth is the men walked out of the fire without a scratch. The ultimate truth is God got his glory. Although there are many stories in the bible where the truth made facts a lie, the point is there is a big difference between a fact and the truth. Lazarus stayed in the tomb for four days presumed dead. But the truth is he was only sleeping for four days. When one is trying to build any relationship, truth must always be on the table. Not facts but truth. Not man's truth, but God's truth. When you build a relationship on facts, there's a strong chance that the very foundation will be shaky. Shaky because if there's ever an opportunity for the truth to show up, it will destroy the foundation. I have learned, from personal experience, that God's truth will completely change everything, and everyone involved. The truth can bring freedom to a situation that one didn't even think needed freedom. There is a power that literally operates in the truth that cannot be denied. A liberty, or eye opener, that impacts everything and everyone it touches. From experience I have learned that the truth can strengthen and build up a relationship, or it can sever a relationship permanently. That's the dangerous thing about the truth. There is nothing that can stop the power of the truth. Good or bad! I remember being married to my son's mother. Now let me briefly explain my personal nature. I can't in any way do fake or phony. I can't act like everything is ok when there is a huge elephant in the room. I can't hide my inner or outer feelings when something is not right. My old pastor, God rest her soul, said Minister Green you need to learn how to control your facial expressions. I said "I can't help it." Right is right and wrong is wrong. Fast forward. There was a time when I was married to my son's mother. We would go through what I call cycles. Which I don't do. Now don't get me wrong. Every marriage has its ups and downs, but the truth is something was wrong. We would handle the situation the way a normal couple would. We would sit and talk like any other couple, adjust to what was said to be the problem and move accordingly. But somehow, we would end up in the same hole. Now although we put all the facts on the table, the truth was something was still wrong. I needed whatever that something was to be brought to the light. Now what else could be brought to the light? We spoke like adults, so there shouldn't have bee any topics to bring to the table. Facts! I say facts because the truth is there was still something seriously wrong. Being a man of the cloth, I knew the only one who could reveal the truth was God. Was I prepared for the truth that would be revealed? No, I was not. Did I think that bringing forth the truth would strengthen our marriage? Yes, I did. So I asked God to reveal to me the truth. What was the true source of the cycle? God revealed to me the true direction of her heart. He said her heart wasn't even in truly fixing the marriage. Her heart was focused on fixing the broken relationship between her and her mother. I was fresh in my walk with God, so I needed to make sure I was truly hearing from God. The word tells us to try the spirit by the spirit to see if it is indeed of God. Was I truly ready for the truth? Definitely not! So I sat her down and began to tell her what I believe God had revealed to me. When I told her, her eyes got as big as quarters. She had the look of busted. That look when something is exposed that was meant to stay hidden. I was both encouraged and devastated all at the same time. Encouraged because I was truly hearing from God himself. Devastated to know where her heart truly was.

Even in the devastated mindset, I still tried to, I guess you could say, reason with her on the behalf of God. I told her the only one who could fix the relationship between her and her mother was God himself. She looked me square in my eyes and said I know it's going to take God to fix it, but I want to do it. If you can acknowledge that the only way a problem can be fixed is by God alone, then to me you're saying the only one who can fix it is God. So technically, if God doesn't fix it, it won't get fixed. I can't understand or see that any other way. And if it's not God's truth, I don't even want to try. So when I heard her say she wanted to do it, something in me immediately shut down. Needless to say, shortly after that we were separated and eventually divorced. Now let's look at the facts here. We loved each other and had an amazing son while we were together. Everything looked normal on the outside. Those were some good looking facts that do mean a lot. Let's look at the truths that over time ultimately led to a divorce. The truth is without God, nothing is ever going to work. The truth is when a person's heart isn't in something, it's a waste of time to expect positive fruit to come forth. God will never go against a person's will, so to expect something productive from no heart is truly defeating the purpose. Knowing the truth can be extremely heartbreaking. Knowing the truth can be extremely uplifting. Although this can happen in any situation, the truth is the only thing that can set a person free.

The truth will always solidify any relationship or situation. The truth is the one foundation one can build on forever. The reason so many people are bound with things like anger, depression, suicide, etc., is because God's truth hasn't been presented to them yet. My life would have gone in a completely different direction had I known God's truth about my life. Knowing the difference between a fact and the truth can be the difference in life or death. God's truth is a price of freedom that has already paid for!

Chapter 8

Why the soul?

Who Exactly Is Doing The Leading?

Why the soul of a woman is a very interesting question? I had the exact same question when I was given the title. When a man first meets a woman and finds her attractive, is this something he thinks about? How often have you heard a man say I want to make love to her soul? And how often do you hear men say her soul sure looks good? Now let's flip it around. When was the last time you heard a woman say I want a man to make love to my soul? How often do you hear women confess he's good for my soul? If you look at the pattern from both sides, you just might see the need for such information. When I received this particular title, I wondered what would be revealed through such a subject.

Well, it didn't take long to start writing. Before Eve took that one bite of the forbidden fruit, she was a perfect being. She was flawless. No hurts, no scars, and no emotional baggage. She was absolutely perfect. Once she took that one bite, she became a completely different being, both naturally, and more importantly, spiritually. Keyword being different. The soul of a human consists of the mind, will, and emotions. This is the area where true change can occur. This is the most important change for both the man and the woman. But in this case, we're talking about the soul of the woman. The soul is the one area where things are the most real and the thing that God cares about the most. He said in his word, *"I wish above all that you prosper, even as your soul prospers."*

Before a person gives themselves to Christ, they are one person. Once he's allowed into the heart and given permission, that person begins to change. They begin to become someone else through the power of God. Now that we know the soul is the most important thing to God, let's try and answer that question from the title. Some people would automatically say that when it comes to a relationship, talking about the soul is being too spiritual. But in all actuality, it's more beneficial than anything. Let's use some balance to get a full understanding of the answer to the question. Because we understand that the soul of a woman is so important, we immediately must understand that doing what's best for her soul, is basically doing what's best for her.

Because we understand that the soul is so important, we immediately understand that for a woman to see and know that the man is genuinely concerned about her soul speaks volumes to her. He's letting her know that he loves her past her flesh. He's letting her know that the most important thing to her is the most important thing to him. Even if she doubted before, she now has a reason to believe that there is a God, and that he must really love her because he sent her a man that is not just concerned about what's between her legs. Faith enhanced!

Of course, we know that the man is not expected to make a daily declaration that her soul is important, but his actions will prove to her that he is genuinely concerned about what is best for her. Making love to her soul is all about what is best for her overall. Now let's look at the flip side to the question. When it comes to making love to the soul, allowing her to experience something she has never experienced before goes far beyond the pleasing of her flesh. This is a time for him to make her feel something far beyond what her mind already knows. Why the soul? The soul is the place where God resides, so pleasing God will definitely please her. Touching something in a woman that has never been touched, is like sending her to the moon and back!

Chapter 9

You Have To Know God

Understandings That Have Been Locked
For Ages

As I was preparing to wrap up the writing portion of this book, I received this particular chapter. While writing the other chapters, I wondered in the back of my mind if God was going to come this way. Being an ordained minister, I guess this would be a normal question. Well, I got my answer. He revealed to me that the reason he waited until the end is because he wanted me to expound on the keys of knowledge for both the male readers and the female readers. Keys that will unlock understandings that have been locked for ages. For the male readers, he said the key to educate on how God intended for the woman to be properly loved from God's perspective. The key to understanding the true nature of a woman and how to connect with her on a spiritual level.

The key to opening up the eyes of the understanding to be able to properly communicate with the woman.

The key to provide the woman with not only what she needs, but is spiritually entitled to. There are also some keys for the woman as well. The key to educate on how God really sees them and how he intended for the woman to be treated. The key to unlocking her eternal potential. Many women have a hidden desire to really be loved the way she is supposed to be. Many women settle for the limitations that the human mind presents. But as all the other chapters have traveled in the direction of the woman, so shall this one. The woman was created a certain way. She was taken from the flesh of man and given her own identity. Now let's look at that created from his flesh element. Because she came from his flesh, and he was all spirit before he fell, she has a certain eternal connection that is generated from the power of God.

This connection allows the man and the woman to connect as a general species. This connection goes far beyond the physical connection, or shall I say the lust of the flesh. This connection resides in a place that can not be seen with the human eye. Nine out of ten women will tell you that they desire more from a man. More than just the physical connection. They may not know how to put it in words, but it's there. This is what they are referring to. This connection is imperative in building any type of foundation to any relationship. When seeking the right relationship with a woman or man, there must be a connection.

Now let's take this a little bit further. We need to fully understand that neither the man nor the woman can force the connection to happen. Some can act as if the connection is there, but deep down inside a true connection cannot be forced. The reason why this connection cannot be forced is because it's a spiritual element, so it has to happen on its own. Some would say predestined to happen. Now, how does one know how to connect with a woman this way? Well, let me start my answer to that question by saying the woman is not going to tell the man how to connect with her.

A woman can tell you some things about herself, like her favorite food or color, but she can't tell you how to connect with her. So how does he know? When a man meets and spends time with a woman, he learns whether or not there is any type of connection. Now there are times when the connection isn't there, but he is really aroused by the presence of this woman. How will he obtain the connection with this woman? The answer is he must seek God. This woman who has now captured his attention and imagination was created by God. God knows everything about this woman, so if the man really wants to be with this woman, he must seek God. Outside of the things that she reveals, God is the only one who can place him on the pathway to her heart.

That pathway to her heart can only be seen through the eyes of his understanding if God allows. Seeking God gives the man two added advantages in obtaining this connection. The first advantage is the most important because it puts man in an eternal position with God. There are two people in this world whom you cannot fool, and that's God and yourself. When a man seeks God for any reason, what God does is search the heart of the matter. When God sees that the heart is pure, he most of the time acts upon a pure heart. If God does reveal anything about the woman to the man, it's because he sees the heart and motives towards the woman. Revealing anything to the man means that God has found the man worthy of such information.

For God to find one worthy in any capacity is an eternal blessing. That means that God has found this man not only worthy to genuinely communicate with God, but also to know valuable things about that woman where in any other situation would not be revealed. This truth alone speaks volumes about the man's heart. Now let's look at the other advantage as the man begins to act upon the things that God has revealed. The woman will automatically know who he has been getting his information from. Now he may run across one of her friends and learn a thing or two and that's okay. The woman has things about herself that she'll never tell a soul. These are the things that make the woman.

When the woman realizes that this man knows things about her that only God knows, she becomes impressed and intrigued. Impressed that this man would go to such great lengths to get to know her on a much deeper level and intrigued as to what else he knows. In her eyes she, if she didn't before, now knows that she cannot only truly trust God, but now she knows that she can trust the man as well because he is hearing from the eternal God. If God can trust him, then so can she!

Chapter 10

Now is time

The Most Precious Thing She Owns

Now this particular chapter comes in last for two reasons. Number one being I had no intentions on touching on the physical side simply because of the title of the book. The second reason is, which is the most important reason, God gave me the title and instructed me to place it last. But if you're familiar with his word, Isaiah 55:8 says his way of doing things are completely different. So I began to meditate on the title of this chapter and found myself writing. As I was meditating, the first thing I found myself thinking about was balance. Because balance is so far from the subject, I really thought I was tripping as they say. But I stayed open to the possibility and learned a few things that I'd like to share.

As The Holy Spirit outlined this topic, I learned and began to understand the mindset of a woman when it comes to her actions in the bedroom. When you talk about the word balance, there's the immediate understanding of two sides. One must understand that there is a big difference between genuine love and the lust of the flesh. The bedroom experience for a woman who is truly in love is always done from the balance of two sides. I learned that these two sides will always be in operation. The beautiful thing about a woman who is truly in love is, she knows both sides are in full operation, and she is extremely emotional about experiencing the two. Unfortunately, this is not something the man will experience, but she will confide in her joys of one side of the scale.

At this point it's all emotional for her. The actual physical act is basically the icing on the cake of what she is already feeling and experiencing. Now it's time to fulfill her emotional and physical appetite with the man whom she has fallen in love with. Now, let's look at one side of the scale. If I had to put a description or specific name on each side of the scale, this particular side, I would call value. Now you wouldn't think that value would even be on the mind at such a time, but for a woman who is truly in love, value is directly on the table. This has been a long time coming because she is in love. Value! Why is value on the table at such a physical time? Shouldn't it be about the physical and nothing else? Not quite when it comes to the thought process of a woman in her heart.

She knows and understands that her physical body is the absolute most precious thing she owns. She knows that giving herself away physically is the most richest thing she can give him. She owns nothing else outside of her heart, that he desires more. She knows and fully understands that the physical parts of her body were specifically designed and created to give the man specific physical, mental, and emotional pleasure. Value! She knows that there is no monetary value that can be placed on what she is physically about to give away.

She's the valuable thing that she is about to give away. Now here's the thing, a woman who is truly in love wants to offer such a valuable treasure to the man she has fallen in love with. She literally wants him to have the best physical part of her. Her heart and mind are already in agreement with giving the body away. She wants him to experience the ultimate value of her body. At this point, he's like a bank or credit union. She is ready to make a deposit that she knows if received right, will change his life forever. Value! She, in her heart and mind, has found him truly worthy of such a deposit, and is now ready to do the actual transfer of the funds. She is ready to open what we call a joint bank account.

The beautiful thing about this joint account is it flows exactly how it's supposed to flow. We know in a normal joint account, both parties have complete, and total access to the entire account. When a woman is truly in love, she knows that the word of God says that her body belongs to the man. She is extremely eager for him to know that in a sense, their journey in finding each other in her mind is complete. In her mind, they have reached the point where there are no more lines to be aware of, no more fearful apprehensions, and no more longing of the flesh. At this point, she needs him to fully understand her value, the value she is bringing to the table, and the value of the deposit she has made in him and in their relationship. Her value is extremely important to her, so now she wants her value to be his possession.

Now, let's take a look at the other side of the scale for a moment. In keeping up with my original statement in this chapter, I would have to call the other side of the scale opportunity. Now just as before, the word opportunity sounds a bit far fetched. After you continue to read, you most definitely will agree with the word opportunity. When we talk about the word opportunity, it too operates in the form of balance. When it comes to opportunity in this case, both the man and the woman have ultimate opportunities that will be conquered during this time. Let's look at the element of opportunity directly from the male's perspective in her mind.

Now that this area is about to be completely secure, she knows that he has been fantasizing about being physical with her, and she knows that there are many things that he wants to do to her and with her. She knows that he has been withstanding the lusts of his flesh, and the fiery darts of the devil with temptation of other women, and most importantly, he has chosen to keep himself pure before God until the ultimate time to be with the woman of his dreams. Now he has the opportunity to not only do what he has been desiring to do, but what he has earned the opportunity to do. Now, lets look at the word opportunity from the woman's perspective. This element of opportunity is pretty similar to that of the man, but just slightly different. The first thing is she is literally ready to forward him the opportunity to do whatever he desires to do. Now the flip side is she also has desires that she has been thinking about constantly as well.

She has a list of things that she, not only wants to do to him, but also a list of things she wants him to do to her. This is an extremely overwhelming time for her because at this exact moment she is like a kid in a candy store. This is the ultimate opportunity for her to explore everything that has crossed her mind. Now their souls will really connect because now there's balance. Now he's making love to her body and her soul.